OLYMPIC NATIONAL PARK

A TRUE BOOK

by

Sharlene and Ted Nelson

Children's Press®
A Division of Grolier Publishing

New York London Hong Kong Sydney
Danbury, Connecticut

Reading Consultant
Linda Cornwell
Learning Resource Consultant
Indiana Department
of Education

Subject Consultant
Michael Smithson
Chief Interpretive Officer
Olympic National Park

Authors' Dedication
To the staff and volunteers
at Olympic National Park

Olympic National
Park's seacoast

Library of Congress Cataloging-in-Publication Data

Nelson, Sharlene P.
    Olympic National Park / by Sharlene Nelson and Ted Nelson.
    p.   cm. —(A true book)
    Includes bibliographical references and index.
    Summary: Describes the landscape, wildlife, and activities of
Washington State's Olympic National Park.
    ISBN: 0-516-20446-7 (lib.bdg.)   0-516-26271-8 (pbk.)
    1. Olympic National Park (Wash.)—Juvenile literature. [1. Olympic
National Park (Wash.) 2. National parks and reserves.] I. Nelson, Ted W.
II. Title. Iil. Series.
F897.O5N45   1997
917.97`980443—dc21   96-39888
                                                                           CIP
                                                                           AC

Contents

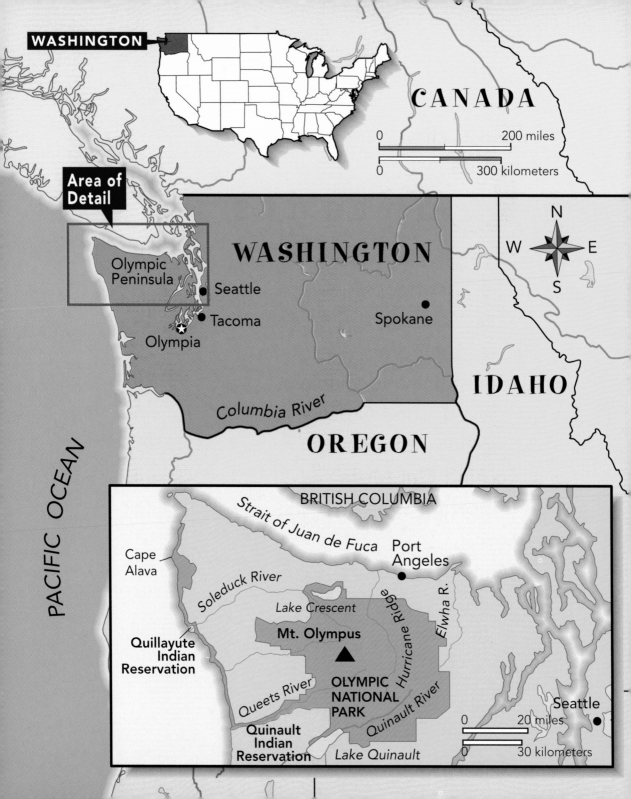

WASHINGTON

CANADA

0 ————— 200 miles

0 ————— 300 kilometers

Area of Detail

WASHINGTON

Olympic Peninsula

Seattle

Tacoma

Spokane

★ Olympia

N
W   E
S

IDAHO

Columbia River

OREGON

PACIFIC OCEAN

BRITISH COLUMBIA

Strait of Juan de Fuca

Cape Alava

Soleduck River

Lake Crescent

Mt. Olympus

Port Angeles

Hurricane Ridge

Elwha R.

Quillayute Indian Reservation

OLYMPIC NATIONAL PARK

Queets River

Quinault River

Quinault Indian Reservation

Lake Quinault

Seattle

0 ——— 20 miles

0 ——— 30 kilometers

Olympic National Park

Olympic National Park is located on Washington's Olympic Peninsula. The park covers almost 1 million acres (405,000 hectares) and is larger than the state of Rhode Island. Rugged, snow-capped mountains, called the Olympic

Mount Olympus is covered with snow throughout the year.

Mountains, rise in the middle of the park. The tallest peak is Mount Olympus. It is nearly 8,000 feet (2,438 meters) high. More than 260 glaciers can be found on the highest peaks of the Olympic Mountains. Rivers that are fed by snow and rain tumble down the mountains. The rivers flow through valleys and forests. At the park's seacoast shore, waves roll in from the Pacific Ocean.

The First People

For thousands of years, the Quileute, Quinault, and Makah American Indians lived in the forests along the coast of the Olympic Peninsula. They used stone tools and cedar trees to build their houses. They carved canoes from cedar logs. They used their canoes to hunt whales and seals.

Stone and wood tools (left) are among the artifacts displayed at a Makah Indian village. Prospectors (right) searched the Olympic Mountains for gold and copper.

In the 1850s, prospectors (people who look for gold, silver, or copper) and trappers traveled into the area. Soon after, settlers arrived. The settlers planted crops in meadows that were in the forest.

The Press Expedition

In 1889, a Seattle newspaper offered to pay for an exploring trip into the Olympic Mountains. It was called the "Press Expedition." Five men, four dogs, and two mules left Port Angeles, Washington, in December.

The members of the Press Expedition hiked in deep snow, climbed mountains, and cut down trees to use as bridges over the rivers. They shot elk for food, but sometimes they had only flour soup to eat.

It took six months for the expedition to reach the Pacific Ocean. Today, summer backpackers can hike the route in about five days.

In 1890, a U.S. army officer led scientists into the area. They discovered large herds of elk. The officer suggested that the Olympic Mountains be made a park to protect the elk from hunters and trappers.

President Theodore Roosevelt created Mount Olympus National Monument in 1909. The herds of elk were named Roosevelt elk, in the president's honor.

In 1937, President Franklin D. Roosevelt visited the monument. He stayed at a lodge on Lake

Theodore Roosevelt (left) and
Franklin D. Roosevelt (right)

Crescent, a large lake on the north side of the mountains. The next year he created Olympic National Park.

The park's seacoast was added to Olympic National Park in 1953. It is a strip of land that is 60 miles (97 kilometers) long.

The Seacoast

Just off the shore from the coastline stand tall seastacks. They are columns of rock that were once part of the mainland. But wind and waves washed the land away, leaving the seastacks behind.

Sandy beaches line the coast. In many places, old

Seastacks (above) are found off the coast of Olympic National Park. Log heaps (right) are a common sight along the beaches.

trees and logs lie in heaps. They were washed ashore by the ocean's waves.

Tide pools are
full of sea life.

There are also rocky beaches with tide pools. Tide pools
are areas of shallow water that
are found among the rocks
when the tide is low. These
small pools can be full of sea
life. Crabs crawl about in the

pools. Green sea anemones wave their tentacles to catch food that is floating by. Seastars dine on barnacles and mussels. Barnacles and mussels are two kinds of sea animals that attach themselves to rocks. Barnacles have only one shell, but mussels have two shells.

Sea otters can be found swimming among the rocks. Seals and sea lions often rest on the rocks before diving

Clockwise from top left: Sea lions prepare to jump into the ocean. A black bear munches on meadow grass. Raccoons usually come out at night to find food, but they can sometimes be seen during the day. A bald eagle takes flight with its freshly caught salmon.

back into the ocean for another swim. Eagles swoop down from the sky to catch salmon in their talons.

Black bears, deer, and raccoons live in the forests that are along the seacoast. Campers who spend the night in the park hang their backpacks from ropes tied to tree branches. Hungry raccoons looking for a midnight snack often raid backpacks that are left on the ground.

The Rain Forest

The park's rain forest grows in river valleys near the seacoast. There, fog drifts in and settles among the trees. Temperatures in the rain forest are mild—not very hot and not too cold.

Storms blow into the park from the sea. As clouds rise to cross the Olympic Mountains,

The rain forest offers comfortable temperatures in which to explore.

rain pours down on the forest below. Each winter, 12 feet (3.7 meters) to 14 feet (4.3 m) of rain falls on the rain forest.

Trees tower over visitors to the rain forest.

Huge trees grow in the rain forest, including Sitka spruce, hemlock, red cedar, and bigleaf maple. Many of these trees are covered with moss. They look like green, hairy giants.

Trees that have been blown down by winds become "nurse logs." As the fallen trees rot, tree seeds sprout on the nurse logs. The seeds grow into tiny new trees called seedlings.

Hundreds of tree seedlings grow on decaying nurse logs.

The seedlings grow and their roots spread over the old log and into the ground.

As the nurse logs continue to rot, the seedlings keep growing into tall trees. After a while, the nurse logs rot away. But the roots of the new trees remain. Because the roots are above the ground, the trees look like they are standing on stilts.

When you explore the trails in the rain forest, you may see

When old logs rot away, the roots of new trees look like stilts.

Roosevelt elk. More than five thousand of these beautiful animals live in Olympic National Park. They roam the park in herds of about ten to one hundred elk.

Roosevelt Elk

Roosevelt elk are a large kind of deer. The males, or bulls, weigh up to 1,000 pounds (454 kilograms). Male Roosevelt elk are about the size of a small horse. Females are a bit smaller than the males.

Every spring, the bulls begin to grow antlers. By late summer, the antlers have many sharp points. The distance between the tip of one antler to the tip of the other antler can be up to 3 feet (91 centimeters)! Every winter, the bulls shed their antlers.

Mountains and Glaciers

Millions of years ago the Olympic Mountains began as a round mound of land that was pushed up from the sea. Rain caused many streams to form in the mound. The streams flowed down the mound and cut gullies in its sides.

Glaciers still cover some of the peaks in the Olympic Mountains.

About two million years ago, the ice ages began. Much of the earth was covered by glaciers. Glaciers are large masses of ice. The glaciers moved slowly, carving the mountains' deep valleys and jagged peaks.

Then, about 12,000 years ago, the earth's climate began to change. The temperature became warmer. The largest glaciers began to melt. Today, scientists believe that two glaciers on Mount Olympus are left over from the last ice age! Some of the other glaciers are about 2,500 years old.

The road to Hurricane Ridge

Your family can drive to
Hurricane Ridge to see some
of the valleys carved by
ancient glaciers. The road up
to Hurricane Ridge winds

31

Visitors can enjoy spectacular views from the Hurricane Ridge Visitor Center.

into the mountains, and through a Douglas fir forest. It passes clearings above the valleys. At the clearings, visitors can get out of their cars to read signs that tell about the glaciers.

At the Hurricane Ridge Visitor Center, you can look through a telescope to see the glaciers on Mount Olympus. While you are there, you might hear a distant whistle. If you do, it may be an Olympic marmot.

Whistlers and Croakers

Marmots are brown, furry animals that are about the size of a small dog. They hibernate in the winter, and scramble from their burrows in the summer. They eat wildflowers, and play, box, and kiss each other!

Olympic marmots live in mountain meadows or on rocky

Olympic marmots are playful, but shy, animals.

slopes. When they sense danger—a red-tailed hawk or a black bear—the marmots whistle a warning to each other. Then they scramble back into their burrows for safety.

Otters are found along the park's rivers.

Many other mammals, birds, reptiles, and amphibians live in Olympic National Park. While you are there, look for river otters, frogs, and great blue herons along the park's rivers.

Great blue herons are large birds with long, skinny legs.

Great blue herons stand on long legs to watch for fish swimming by in the water.

They stand in the water as still as statues. When they see a small fish, they spear it with their beaks and gulp the fish down. Then, croaking loudly, they flap their 6-foot-wide (2 meters) wings and fly to another spot to continue fishing.

Exploring the Park

Most of Olympic National Park is wilderness. There are no roads, buildings, or large crowds of people to disturb the wild animals and plants. But there are still easy ways to explore this beautiful park.

A highway loops around and through the lowland areas

of the park. From the highway, roads lead to the seacoast, rain forest, mountains, and to the beginning of the trails.

The Hall of Mosses got its name from the long moss that hangs from huge trees.

There are more than 500 miles (800 km) of trails through Olympic National Park. There are long trails

that lead into the mountains'
wilderness. There are also
short, easy trails that lead to
interesting places such as the
rain forest's "Hall of Mosses."

A stop at the park's main
visitor center will help you
decide which roads and trails
to explore. The main visitor
center is located in Port
Angeles, on the road to
Hurricane Ridge. There you'll
find displays, maps, and
schedules for summer park

Visitors are dwarfed
by a giant Douglas fir.

Some visitors have close encounters with the park's wildlife.

programs to help you learn more about the park.

Exploring the natural wonders of Olympic National Park will surely be an experience you'll never forget.

43

To Find Out More

Here are some additional resources to help you learn more about Olympic National Park:

 **Books**

 **Organizations**

Georges, D. V. **Glaciers.** Childrens Press, 1986.

Hallett, Bill and Jane Hallett. **National Park Service: Activities and Adventures for Kids.** Look & See, 1991.

Lepthien, Emilie U. **Elk.** Childrens Press, 1994.

Mead, Robin. **Facts America: Our National Parks.** Smithmark, 1993.

National Park Service
Pacific Northwest Region
909 First Avenue
Seattle, WA 98104-1060

Olympic National Park
600 East Park Avenue
Port Angeles, WA 98362

Olympic Park Institute
111 Barnes Point Road
Port Angeles, WA 98362
E-mail: opi@olympus.net

Port Angeles Chamber of Commerce
121 East Railroad
Port Angeles, WA 98362

Online Sites

Olympic National Park

*http://www.halcyon.com/
rdpayne/onp.html*

History, photos, schedules, facts and figures, and links to other sites within the park, plus information on wildlife, vegetation, geology, camping, food, places to stay, ranger stations, and picnic areas.

National Park Service: Olympic National Park

*http://www.nps.gov/
parklists/index/olym.html*

News about the park, general information, statistics, and links to other sites.

Glaciers in Olympic National Park

*http://sequim.sequim.com/
park/glaciers.html*

Everything you want to know about these vast masses of snow and ice: their structure, activity, variety, glacier climbing, and more.

Great Outdoors Recreation Pages (GORP): Olympic

*http://www.gorp.com/gorp/
resource/US_National_
Park/wa_olymp./html*

A lot to see and learn: park descriptions, history, photos, marine life, the mountains, the giant trees of the forest, visitor information, and a bookstore.

Olympic National Forest

http://www.olympus.net/onf/

Recreation opportunities, general information, addresses, history of the forest, and links to other sites.

Important Words

burrow hole or tunnel dug in the ground by an animal

gully long, narrow ravine or ditch

hibernate to sleep deeply during the winter

lowland land at the base of a mountain

moss furry green plant that grows on damp soil, rocks, and tree trunks

talons the sharp claws of a bird, such as an eagle, a falcon, or a hawk

tide change in sea level caused by the pull of the sun and the moon on the Earth

Index

Meet the Authors

Sharlene and Ted Nelson's home overlooks Washington's Puget Sound and the Olympic Mountains. They have hiked many of the trails in Olympic National Park, and enjoy camping on the park's beaches with their grandchildren.

Sharlene and Ted Nelson have been exploring the Pacific North-west for more than thirty years, and have written many articles and books about the area for both children and adults. Their most recent True Book title for Children's Press is *Mount St. Helens National Volcanic Monument.*

Photographs ©: David J. Forbert: 15 inset, 22, 43; James P. Rowan: 15 top, 31; Janis Burger: 2, 10, 29, 37, 39; National Park Service, Olympic National Park: 25; Olympic National Park: 6, 9, 11 top, 13, 32, 35; Pat O'Hara: 1, 16, 41, 42; Photo Researchers: 21 (Michael P. Gadomski), 18 top right (Calvin Larsen), 27 (Tom & Pat Leeson), 23 (Gary Retherford); Tom & Pat Leeson: cover, 11 bottom, 18 top left, 18 bottom right, 18 bottom left, 26, 36.